SATURDAY MORNING SEROTONIN

Poems by

NINA BELÉN ROBINS

Thompson & Columbus, Inc., Publishers
New York

Published by Thompson & Columbus, Inc.

ISBN: 979-8-9869385-2-3

Cover and Book Design
Mark Wedemeyer / Carbon13 Design Bureau
Select cover elements from Freepik

ninabelenrobins.com

DEDICATED TO

Austin Powers, Wayne Campbell, Charlie Mackenzie, and Shrek who got me through some of the worst times I've had, all by giving me feel good chemicals from laughter before I knew what that was.

CHOOSE YOUR OWN ANALOGY

Comedy Central :: depression
comedy reels :: Covid
late shows :: insomnia
talk shows :: staying home from school
stoned movies :: late night baking
tear jerkers :: pms
rom coms :: breakups
movies :: a first date
sitcoms :: unwinding after work
reality shows :: too much drama in your life
Netflix binging :: relationships
cooking shows :: insatiable hunger
screens :: our life

❖

So what do you do to cope with reality?
What screen do you watch?
Which mirror do you choose?
Time of day?
Alone or with someone?

Because there's a screen for it all to
lose yourself in an alternate reality,
since life is unscripted and
none of us have time for that.

ALSO BY NINA BELÉN ROBINS

Supermarket Diaries

A Bed With My Name On It

T. Gondii

Warm Blooded Tree

Ode to Dymphna

CONTENTS

SATURDAY MORNING SEROTONIN

PREFACE

finding fun in your alone time

PEPPER MILL

Dear nine-inch unicorn magnum pepper mill:

You are the grind I never knew I wanted.
Entice me with your thick, long,
high-capacity cylindrical opening.
I never knew I needed so much space
for grinding,
and I grind.
Mix you with my exotic Himalayan pink sea salt.
Twist your extra large steel mechanism
with a bottom thumb screw
until I'm satisfied with your ejection.
You know what hungry women want:
something to grip onto while we salivate.
I wanna toss my salad with you.
My eggs are waiting.
Go huge, or leave the party.
You take up all my fingers,
fill my grip.
I want to grind you on my clams,
screw your gears in the morning,
rub your smooth at night.
I want to fill you with batteries
and pepper.
I want to taste what you can spew.
I saw you advertised on TV,
as I sat alone, with a bowl
of naked unseasoned snacks,
the only companion I have late at night
when there's no one around.
I always thought unicorns were mythical,
never knew the smooth horns were sold
at Williams Sonoma

hidden among your cheaper imitations.
Forty-five dollars for a pepper mill!
Forty-five dollars for seeds in my mouth.
I keep you on the shelf,
you blend into the corner,
they don't see you.
When I'm lonely, and somber,
eating breakfast by myself,
my apartment silent without passion,
I sweat you in my robe.
Hold you and twist you,
my hands never empty,
you spew on my command.
You stop when I'm finished and
satisfied with spice.
I put you back,
your expulsion
lingering on my tongue,
sharp pleasure vibrating
through this body,
filling the empty void.
My passionate nine-inch pepper mill.
Unicorn magnum.
Big, strong, long, just keep going,
never break.
On Amazon, I promise
I'll give you five stars.

THE POEMS

get that dopamine

SUPERMAN GOES TO THERAPY

I know I don't usually ask you to talk last minute like this;
make these emergency appointments.
You never thought I needed therapy.
I save lives, am faster than a speeding bullet.
Why would you think I need saving?

I can't take the crying anymore,
the sleepless nights.
I'm a baby monitor for the world,
there is no one to share the responsibility.
I want to spend the night with Lois,
spoon for eight hours,
kiss her lips while she is sleeping.
She will always come second;
there is always someone who needs me more.

I wish I needed Clark's glasses,
couldn't see all the bad in the world.
My cape is worn.
Clark's pajamas and blue jeans
are much more comfortable.
I don't need these muscles
or spandex to show them off.
I am fine with sweatpants sometimes,
five o'clock shadow,
unbrushed hair.
I want to wake up at ten am on a Saturday
with no thought of the afternoon's evil.

I know this may seem crazy
but I am thinking kryptonite.
Not to die, not to suffer,
just enough to take out the super from me;
the otherworldliness.

You are a doctor, you can figure out the dose.
Take this super strength, super hearing, speed.
I am fine with normal, human.

I want the voices to stop crying.
I don't mention the ones I cannot save,
cannot get to.
Everyone thinks there's only one at a time.
There are thousands:
tears and screams.
I can hear them all.

Give me kryptonite.
Take these eardrums out.
I can't continue saving.
Lois needs me, The Daily Planet.
I want to walk among the average
with Clark Kent as my only identity.
I want to blend into the masses
like everyone else.
Take these powers
your sun leaves me
with golden rock.
Never give them back.
I need to rest.
Close my eyes and tune out everyone.
Wake up as Clark
as though this Kryptonian
never lived
on any other world.

BOY

Somewhere, there is a man
who bought
the VERY first ever issue of
Fantastic Four
from the awkward kid
up the street
for a nickel.

An awkward kid who didn't have
Joe DiMaggio baseball cards,
or signed baseballs,
or Saturday afternoons
playing catch with his dad
like the guy he sold it to.
Just a bedroom
where he got to hang out
with Superman and
The Flash.

His mom and dad
downstairs wondering,
What's wrong with this boy
that he doesn't have friends?
It must be the comics,
better make them leave.

They didn't see the belt
tied to the back of a chair
and around his neck
those three afternoons,
the bullies in
the yard at school,

super heroes swooping down
to save him.

Just a bookshelf
filled with comic books
emptied
in one afternoon.

Superman kicked out
of the bedroom,
The Flash sold
to the kid next door,
Fantastic Four
spread out on another table.

A boy clinging to a cliff,
a window.
Flashing a Batman
signal.
Fifty nickels in his pockets
dragging him down
toward the waves.

EVERYONE LOVES FREE PIZZA

Planet Fitness appreciates
your donation today.
One dollar to start,
ten dollars a month.

The buff man behind the counter
takes your credit card and bank account.

Planet Fitness appreciates
your momentum and dedication.

Planet Fitness knows
that we all want to be
societally beautiful,
but the gym is a nuisance,

so when I show up,
tell them I've lost one hundred pounds
in less than a year
their mouths hit the counter.

How did you do that?
How on earth is that possible?
Gym employees never witnessing
daily workouts at the gym.

The business model at Planet Fitness
assumes you will only show up
for free pizza day,
stay comfortable in your skin.
That despite society,

despite the pressure,
we are all mostly OK
living in our bodies.

AMAZING AMAZON

The condo complex has requested
the tenants crush their cardboard
as everyone has become
addicted to Amazon and
online stores, the rush of
It's been shipped emails.

The dumpster is overflowing,
the HOA can only
afford so many dump trucks.

We have been trapped at home,
searching for whatever relief from this.

As I have shrunk I have become addicted
to clicking checkout on the websites.

How the sites like reminding me:
People your size typically wear a size small.

My internet is flooded with cookies
replacing the cookies I gave up.

Boxes at the front door of jeans and pajamas.
A closet of clothes sized huge to tiny.
My complex mates coping with isolation
by filling up landfills,

me filling an empty stomach
with a lessened bank account.
A full dresser drawer.
The fabricated satisfaction of less fabric,
a hole in my savings account
paying for a false sense of self worth.

BE LIKE BARBIE!

Barbie can be anything she wants
when we are six.

Barbie probably got straight A's
in her prestigious school.
Barbie got accepted
to medical school,
law school,
Harvard.

Barbie has never heard no.

Give us girls our inspiration!
Give us girls hope!
That is what Barbie is for.

Barbie never gets weight loss surgery
because she has the best metabolism.
Barbie doesn't need meds!
She has perfect metabolics.
Barbie has never checked into rehab,
she doesn't have an addictive personality!

But she's a role model!
Be like Barbie!

Barbie has never had an abortion
because her birth control is 100%!
Barbie has never keyed her ex-boyfriend's car
because Ken never cheats!

Be like Barbie!
Be a lawyer!
Be a doctor!
Be flawless!

Because she is our role model!
Because our role model never fails!
Because role models are the most realistic!
Because the only way to succeed
is to never mess up!

MAKEOVER MONTAGE

Teen movies in the 90's
hate glasses and messy hair.
Montages of pop music fix that.
Wardrobe raids and makeup.

I fluctuate in weight,
mustache, hairstyle.

The ladies at the eyebrow salon
beg me to come more
than once a month;
I tip them 30% to compensate.

Physical beauty is meaningless
but I know how to get it,
I just hate putting in the work.

I don't have a bunch of
girlfriends to sit me down
in front of a vanity,
just occasional threading,
hair brushing.

But the way the people react
when I tend to them,
I feel like I am missing something
without the pop music
in the bathroom,
without Freddy Prince Jr.
waiting at the bottom of the stairs,

knowing exactly how ugly
they all think I am
before I remove my glasses.

MIRRORS AND PHOTOGRAPHS

The comedian on stage
wants you to know that up until this year
he was ugly and wasted his youth
developing his personality.

He asks girls to make viral videos
about how they want to sleep
with him because of his muscles
and posts it on TikTok.

The comedian brags about his penis
because now he's hot enough
that all the girls in the audience
are visualizing it.

On Facebook I post the pictures
of before I looked like this because
I'm the best I've ever been and I know it.
Because up until this year I was ugly
so I developed a personality.

Matt Rife probably wonders
how early he would have lost his virginity
if his jawline had always been angled like this
and I wonder how many men
I would have slept with
if my dresses always fit like this.

So we get on stage or social media
and show the world how hot we are now,
looking in every window and mirror,
obsessing and asking for validation.

While our old mirror reflections
cry and hate and sulk.
While our old photos
fall, defeated, into a bottom drawer,
only to be shown now
that our appearance is acceptable.
Now that we are worthy of the camera lens.

SUNDAY SERATONIN

no one realized
in the 90's
about animal videos
and serotonin
but there we were
on sundays
watching videos
and bob saget
who between
full house and
america's funniest home videos
was the country's
serotonin dealer
youtube is here now
so there's that
and we love it
but we still crave
sunday america
how we were all addicts
and yes we've found
substitutes
but like any recovering
user we still fantasize
about it
how we as a collective
sat at our tv's at the end of
the week
after the hell of work
school
kids or relationships
pain
and there was saget
with our fix
that we still crave

that still mends things
animals failing
kids failing
humans failing
levels in our glands rising
as we float into the reality
it is not just us
who are fallible

BINGEWORTHY

Even when I can't watch a movie,
I can watch *Law and Order*,
and it confuses my husband.

Romcoms have bad parts,
comedies have conflict,
dramas make you cry,
even Bambi's mother dies,

but forty-five minutes of murder,
blood on the floor, and
culprits is so easy.

He'll ask me how I cried
at Lady and the Tramp
but don't take a bathroom break
for the rape victim.

How I won't enter a movie theater
but watch marathons of
decapitation on my day off.

Half an hour into it
it's the wrong guy.

After the second commercial break
I can sometimes figure it out.

The good guys start losing
at two thirds in but I don't give up hope.

I just hold on until four minutes before the hour,
sitting on my couch.

Thirty seconds before the credits
I get my answer,
the music comes on, Dick Wolf appears,

then right into another episode
before I can try to remember
how the previous one began.

FEAR THE WALKING LAST OF US

What if the bipolars
are immune to zombies?

We are already zombies
from the meds.
What if we are our own
defense mechanism?

Take the medicine
lose the personality;
for once useful, safe.

Human after human is bitten.
They are weak.
We have walked as though
dead since the first
psych appointment,
since the pharmacy,
the first night with no sleep.

We are the walking dead,
the true last of us.
We have always
wandered only half alive.

Bitten by our own brains
which hate us from the start.

Outsmart and outlive
the sane ones.
It takes an apocalypse
for us to be so high functioning.

SO RELATABLE

The Office television show cast Holly
to be HR and to be a love interest.
She and Michael Scott fall in love,
but there is a subplot.

Dwight tells her Kevin is special needs.
I'm not sure if Kevin is actually
special needs but I do notice he and
I have similarities.

Since Holly thinks Kevin is special needs
she is certainly kinder to him,
so, of course, Kevin thinks she loves him.

The moment in the episode when
Kevin realizes Holly thinks he's
mentally challenged I turn off the television.

Suddenly I'm Kevin.
Suddenly all the people who have loved me are Holly.
Suddenly my jokes about being
the special needs hire at my job
are a script in a comedy series.

They are all so kind to me at work.
They are all so forgiving.
But they are Holly and I am Kevin.

At what point does the self aware
disabled person realize they
were not quite self aware?

When I am sitting on the couch
watching *The Office*,
realizing the show has scripted
all parties involved.

EVERYONE LOVES JESSIE SPANO

I'm so excited!
And I just can't hide it!
I'm so excited!
I'm so scared!

And so were we
and none of us had
tried speed yet
or weed.

Two years later
the first of us lit up,
we were scared for them.

Two years later so did everyone else,
eventually we all
made friends with addiction.

And oh how twenty years later
the cast of *Saved by the Bell*
made a mockery
of that episode.

Oh how they forgot
the ten-year-olds
holding their breath
during an after school special.

And how we forget our own breath.
How Zach hugged Jessie,
threw out the pills,
and each of us
thought we'd be sober forever.

SAFE SPACE FOR THE FORGOTTEN

The free craft and cooking network
has programs with chefs
like Martha Stewart,
or Ming Tsai,
Pati's Mexican Kitchen,
or *Cooking with Julia Child,*

starring an old, bent
forgetting woman
co-hosting
with young guest chefs
star-struck
to share the kitchen.

She'll stand there, amazed

How do you know
how much butter to add?
How did you know to cut
the fruit so well?

Her forgotten art
re-taught by home cooks
with a half pity
reserved for
forgetful grandmothers.

A free network
that gives second chances
to famous chef icons
old and blank.

BETTER THAN SKINEMAX

We want to ask Anne Burrell
to do a late-night
erotica aphrodisiac cooking show.

Tell us Anne,
about chocolate and strawberries,
the avocado mousse
and what we'd do with it.

On *Worst Cooks in America*
she lets it ooze out
before they cut to commercial,
but after ten pm it'd be alright.

Tattooed and dirty
in the kitchen.

I'd stay up for it.
For bananas and honey.
Basil and pine nuts.

Make that pesto.
We'll be here in our pajamas.

We stay up all night
drafting the letter.

Dear Anne,
We want you to enjoy yourself.
We will stay up to see this.
Who needs skinemax
when you can make an arugula
salad with olive oil.
Figs and goat cheese.

Holding bulging bellies
and pudgy hands.
Watching until we fall asleep.

SNAPPLE APPLE

Snapple Apple zero sugar
tastes more like apples than an apple

Snapple Apple zero sugar
has no juice

Snapple Apple zero sugar
makes its debut in New York

Snapple Apple zero sugar
is on discount

Snapple Apple zero sugar
is made with 0 percent real apples

Snapple Apple zero sugar
wants you to forget that

Snapple Apple zero sugar
wants you to taste how apple-y it can be

Snapple Apple zero sugar
has natural flavoring

Snapple Apple zero sugar
wants you to forget that natural flavoring is not natural

Snapple Apple zero sugar wants you to forget
what real juice tastes like

Snapple Apple zero sugar
comes in a six-pack

Snapple Apple zero sugar
tastes best from the fridge

Snapple Apple zero sugar
gets under your tastebuds

Snapple Apple zero sugar
gets into your brain

Snapple Apple zero sugar
has no real fruit juice but you'll forget that

but you'll forgive Snapple Apple zero sugar
because *damn.*

It tastes more like apples
than any apple ever could.

MCDONALDS

The meds told me
I needed twenty chicken nuggets
so I got a few dollars
together and walked
to McDonald's.

Here in NYC it's open
all night
so I stand in line
with the strung outs
and the other kids.

Mom says it's fine
when I walk around
in the middle of the night.
I'm two-hundred-fifty pounds
so no one'll bother me.

The cop over at the table
is trying to coax
a lady out of her pile
of runs on the seat
and all twelve of us start to watch.

Go home he says
but her face falls further
into her hamburger,
brown spilling onto the seat.

Three people leave
and the cop continues.
You can't be here,
where do you live?

She nods into her coke.
The spill seeping into her
holed up sneakers.

I grab my nuggets and walk home.
Lithium makes you care more
about the hunger
than the environment.

In the morning,
a couple sits
at the shit-table
inhaling coffee
and processed egg.

The cop back in his routine,
everyone else asleep.
A scene a
memory only for a dozen.

A bleached table
silently hiding
a spill.

ICE CREAM

I guess the ice cream monger at Carvel
doesn't need to know
I was unaware of the peanut butter ice cream.

The special blend of peanut butter
with vanilla in the soft serve.

How I didn't know about it, now it's gone.
The one flavor they haven't brought back.

I heard it's better than all the other seasonal flavors.
Isn't it, Husband. Isn't it better.

The Carvel ice cream monger just wants to give me my
Rocky Road ice cream with peanut butter syrup.
My so-called substitution.

When your husband cheats on you
I bet it's with a woman.
There are photos to stalk, texts to read.

Last year my husband fell in love
with peanut butter ice cream.

Secret delicious peanut butter ice cream
I will never get to taste.

The affair I'm only mad about
because I wasn't asked to join.

CRAVING DOPAMINE

Fettuccine carbonara brings dopamine,
notifications bring dopamine,
it's all dopamine.
The reels the internet shows me
of carbonara bring dopamine,
and calling the pizza place and ordering salad
reduces dopamine
so I watch more videos of Italian chefs
mixing eggs and parmesan cheese
together to get dopamine.

Everyone likes to talk
about how drugs are so dangerous,
how nicotine is the most addictive chemical,
there are videos on the internet
that drinking a few drinks
every weekend can alter your brain chemistry.

What really changes your brain chemistry
is seeing cream drip off a fork due to algorithms,

and I wonder
do drug addicts see videos of people getting high?
Do alcoholics see videos of drinks being mixed?
At this point,
after months of cream dripping off of forks,
how do I tell Facebook I can't take it anymore?
How do I tell my phone this is not helping?
How do I put down the social media
and go just one full day
without thinking about butter and cream
just to get that fix of dopamine?

VIRAL FELINES

Who loves internet cats?
We love internet cats!
Who follows Instagram cats?
We follow Instagram cats!
Who checks the stories of Instagram cats?
We check the stories of Instagram cats!
Who purchases shirts of Instagram cats?
We purchase shirts of Instagram cats!
Who cares about Instagram cats?
We care about Instagram cats!

Instagram cats are in our living room!
Instagram cats are in our phones!
Instagram cats bring us fuzzies and warm!
Instagram cats get shared in our DM's!
Instagram cats have wonderful lives!
Instagram cats have life spans!

Instagram cats have vet bills.
Who donates to cat go fund me's?
We donate to cat go fund me's!
Who checks in at the vet?
Instagram cats check in at the vet!

Who looks at cat updates?
We look at cat updates!
Who worries when there are no updates for a week?
We worry when there are no updates for a week!
Who posts the cat is so sick?
They post the cat is so sick!

Who cries, whose heart breaks,
whose fingers shake on the screen?
Our fingers tremble and shake on the screen.

Who holds each other in comfort
when they cross the rainbow bridge?
We hold each other in comfort
when they cross the rainbow bridge.

Who scours Instagram to find new cats?
We scour Instagram to find new cats!
Who finds cats to love?
We find cats to love!
Who loves internet cats?
We love internet cats!

JUST AN ONSCREEN ROMANCE

I don't know if you've ever fallen in love with
a movie character.
I hadn't until I saw *Mary Poppins Returns,*

met Jack, with his
perfect cockney accent
charming smile, dance moves.

So I've been cheating
on my husband with this man
during emotional times:
PMS, after a hard day at work,
after some kittens died, a fight.

Under the blanket, but really in the streets
of London, lighting the lamps
with the leery.

Lin-Manuel Miranda!
My sister exclaims
Yes he is very charming!

So I google this man, am so excited
to find clips of him on YouTube.

But I am aghast!
He is NOT cockney, not a leery!
our beloved London just a movie set.

So I ban myself from
Googling this man ever again,
put back the movie, fall asleep
to songs about London
until my husband comes home.

I turn it off reminding myself
there is no other man.
Just a character.

Cuddle with my love.
Admit nothing.

THE ANGRY MASTURBATOR SPEAKS

The awkward thing is buying dildos at Spencer's
if you were curious.

Dildos in the back, kids shopping in the front.
So you sneak to the sex section like it's no big deal.

We all do it. Don't pretend you haven't.
Cheap things, break a month in.
Bed end tables refurbished vibrator graveyards.

If you confide this in the cashier,
vibrator hidden in your fist,
quietly agreeing to overpriced batteries,
they dub you Angry Masturbator.

You, destroyer of eggs,
pocket rockets.
War on batteries.
Amazon woman.

Not angry masturbator
you whisper in your room,
alone with the toys,
husband downstairs.

Warrior woman.
Amazonian.

As if they don't know
they break so easily
to keep you cumming back
for more.

PANTS MAN

On Broadway
by Urban Outfitters
the gray haired homeless man's
pants are by his ankles
in the cross walk,
so we try to avoid
the taxis
turning the curve,
but moreso
this man's rear end,

round
and visible
as he is half bent
and leaning toward
the buildings
and the whole crowd
hurries past,
heaving at the sight.

Across the street are
three girls smoking
by the entrance
with their straightened hair,
designer sunglasses,
five-dollar coffees they got
three blocks prior.

Rocking those new pants they sell,
the ones with the price tags
charging you for holes,
and not material.

The ones that let your butt cheeks
peer out from underneath the belt loops.

We barely notice,
while the men cross over
to the shade splayed
out beneath the building.
Drooling at the sight.

ONLY IF YOU'RE HAPPY

trader joe's hires only happy cheerful people/if you're a happy cheerful person come work for trader joe's/and we'll pay you ten dollars an hour/and give you benefits/and you can be happy/and you can dance/and you can deal with the public/but only if you're happy/and you can give out samples/and deal with the public/but only if you're happy/so come work for trader joe's/and we'll have you do overnight stock/and come in early/and stay late/and yes, sometimes customers are nasty/so only come work here if you're happy/and sometimes we'll cut your hours/but maybe give you full time/if you're happy/if you want your career in a supermarket/just make sure that you're happy/and sometimes you'll burn out/and sometimes you'll get yelled at/and you can be a cashier!/but only if you're happy/because everyone wants to work in a supermarket/because it's always a first choice/so make sure you're happy/so you can work at trader joe's/because it would never be a last resort/to make money/and we pay ten dollars an hour!/so make sure you're happy!/fill out the application!/and you can work at trader joe's/make sure you wake up every morning ready to take on the day!/and just stay happy/or else we'll fire you/and you can go work for some other supermarket/and who would want to/they are sad in other supermarkets/they are tired/they are human/so come work for trader joe's!/and paint that smile on/and we'll hire you!/but only if you're happy!

TO MY DEAREST KIM KARDASHIAN,

I know you keep me on the payroll
to make you look like a mannequin.
Same plastic smile, lips parted
plastic body tanned perfectly,
hair in place, every man's perfection.
I have your angles memorized.
Know your good side like you don't have a bad one.

When I caught you smiling
I almost didn't have my camera ready.
I knew you didn't think anyone could see you
giggling, grinning and glowing.
You looked so real, so human.

I wonder how you are going to react
when you see your giggle on the newsstands.
I wonder if your glow will make you feel vulnerable.
You are so accustomed to your mask of hardness
your softness has no chance to speak out.

Your humanization was almost missed,
my camera almost didn't catch it.
But I have glimpsed this
and I will share it with the world.

You are so real, so actual
even though you insist
on looking at the camera,
still and icy chilled.

EPILOGUE

we are all ok
in the end

DANNON

Oh Dannon
oh maker of steadfast coffee yogurt
vanilla
you were the original
the staple
but in the '90s
the other yogurt companies
began making far more complex flavors
and options
you desperately tried to keep up
with Light + Fit,
and Oikos
but still always fell short
with creativity and taste.

Your marketers tried every tactic.
Every enticing commercial,
promise of weight loss
health etc.

You kept trying
until you came to your final
brilliant idea
of promoting a tasty
fruity
cure for constipation!

Oh Dannon
with your Activia
and tasty laxative
and Jamie Lee
and soccer mom
and supermarket

Oh Dannon with your probiotic
and your perfectly measured
ingredients
to not make explosive diarrhea,
just enough to bring relief,
you found a tasty way
to empty oneself
while still enjoying
a reduced calorie
calcium and protein filled
lunch.

So perfect, so enticing
but brilliant still
was your recent employment
of the desirable and sexy Shakira
as your spokesperson.

Oh Dannon you brilliant schemer!
You letting us know that even the sexy people
become constipated!
Sit on the loo
in frustration.
That even the naked
sweaty
sex goddesses
of the world
desire loose stools
and regulation.

Because that is what's important in life
to the normal, everyday people,
why the Enquirer
posts pictures of cellulite

and celebrity breakups are blown
out of reasonable proportions.

All we want
is to feel sexy.
Feel that our problems are not
something to be embarrassed by.
And now we do,
despite the clogged
colons of the general population.
We buy your yogurt
and feel confident
in our regularity,
because now we even feel sexy
on the john!

GLOSSARY

1. PEPPER MILL
   A large pepper mill with a phallic name inspired this poem.

2. SUPERMAN GOES TO THERAPY
   As Millennials have all been in therapy our whole lives, it would never seem out of the ordinary that a superhero would also have been.

3. BOY
   This actually is about one of the original comic book nerds from the 50's, before it was cool to be a comic book nerd.

4. EVERYONE LOVES FREE PIZZA
   Planet Fitness is a gym that prides itself on no judgment and that anyone can join, therefore everyone with ten dollars joins and none of them go.

5. AMAZING AMAZON
   We are the generation of internet shopping, and apparently killing off all the department stores from previous eras. We are the reason brick and mortar stores are going out of business. Hell, you can get clothes from anyone on Amazon. I have numerous cat shirts from random stores on there.

6. BE LIKE BARBIE!
   Well, the movie came out so how was I not supposed to write the poem?

7. MAKEOVER MONTAGE
   For a good decade, every movie directed at pre-teens and teenagers had makeover scenes almost identical to each other, with music montages, where a bunch of "popular hot girls" would take the "non-popular, non-hot girl" and make her "hot" by taking her glasses off and changing her hair and clothes. It was part of their ploy to have good movie soundtracks of which we all wound up buying the tapes and CD's.

8. MIRRORS AND PHOTOGRAPHS

Matt Rife is a very popular comic who randomly transformed recently from what he considered to be "ugly" to "hot". It's one of his most common bits. It's just as foreign to him as it's been to me to feel this way.

9. SUNDAY SEROTONIN

America's Funniest Home Videos is a television show that used to air on Sunday nights where people would submit their funny home videos and it would be half an hour of watching them, followed by audience votes on which were the funniest. The best one would win a cash prize. *Full House* is a sitcom that we all watched on Friday nights about three guys raising three girls, and it was probably one of the most wholesome television shows of its time.

10. BINGWORTHY

Law and Order is a show that has been on for decades, about cops arresting people, and then lawyers trying them. It is made up of a predictable plot line, just the people and stories change. But every episode goes in the same order, and it is very comforting to watch because there are no surprises.

11. FEAR THE WALKING LAST OF US

This is about the two major zombie apocalypse television shows that have been on recently. A person becomes a zombie by being bitten by one. It is portrayed as a virus that takes over the world, and the last people left have to survive somehow.

12. SO RELATABLE

The Office is a spinoff on a show from Great Britain by the same name. It is a mock reality show of people working in an office. It portrays the day to day life of being at the job, and is fairly realistic and hilarious. I think everyone can relate to at least one of the characters.

13. EVERYONE LOVES JESSIE SPANO

Saved by the Bell was a very popular show in the 90's about kids who were in first middle school, then high school. The main characters were a bunch of really good friends. Mostly it was a lot of fun, but the episode where Jessie got addicted to caffeine pills is the most famous, and the cast still will "replay" the episode whenever they reunite.

14. SAFE SPACE FOR THE FORGOTTEN

Julia Child was the first cooking show star, the first expert. But eventually age hits us all and she forgot her craft.

15. BETTER THAN SKINEMAX

Anne Burrell is a food network star who hosts a food game show called "*Worst Cooks in America*". She is always very sexual and you can tell it's a rebellion. We just want her to do it legally.

16. SNAPPLE APPLE

Snapple Apple is a juice beverage by the company Snapple.

17. MCDONALDS

Everyone from every walk of life eats at McDonalds. In the middle of the night all bets are off for who winds up sitting at the tables.

18. ICE CREAM

Carvel is an ice cream parlor which serves a plethora of different flavors, and seasonally they have a special limited edition flavor in both soft serve and hard ice cream.

19. CRAVING DOPAMINE

Reels are the Millennial version of TikTok, both of which show minute long videos of things you are interested in. But even we are considered old for watching them. We have reels, and the next generation thinks we are "old" and only use TikTok. Who knows what the generation after them will use.

20. VIRAL FELINES
The internet is for cats.

21. JUST AN ONSCREEN ROMANCE
Mary Poppins Returns is the latest remake of an older movie. I'm sure some people think it's blasphemous but it actually is a very good movie, and if you haven't watched it I'd recommend it wholeheartedly.

22. THE ANGRY MASTUBATOR SPEAKS
Spencer's is a store that sells novelty items, with a special section in the back for adults. It's always very embarrassing to shop from the back wall, but sometimes things are necessary.

23. PANTS MAN
Urban Outfitters is a clothing store, and sometimes people like wearing pants that show everything, but I am pretty sure the clothing companies make the pants to save money on material.

24. ONLY IF YOU'RE HAPPY
Trader Joe's is a very trendy supermarket, where the employees are absurdly always in a good mood, which is difficult to understand until you apply for the job and look on the website where they specifically state they prefer happy people in their job force.

25. KIM KARDASHIAN
Kim Kardashian is a famous person. She's always very plastic in photos, but one time I saw a magazine cover in which she was giggling.

26. DANNON
Activia yogurt is a yogurt created specifically for gut health. How could I not write a poem about bathroom humor after seeing Shakira dancing because her bowel movements were finally normal.

ACKNOWLEDGMENTS

I would like to acknowledge Dion Calabro, the love of my life, who has kept me laughing for ten years, and who tolerates the six movies I have the ability to watch, while going to the movie theater by himself because I can't handle the bad parts. Dion also inspired half the poems in this book, if you're an artist marry your biggest fan because they will end up also being your muse.

"Pepper Mill" was first published in *Vanilla Sex Magazine*

"Boy" was first published in *FreezeRay Poetry*

"McDonald's" and "Pants Man" were first published in *Anti-Heroin Chic*

"Angry Masturbator" was first published in *Buck Off Magazine*

"Ice Cream" was first published in *Artistic License*

PRAISE FOR *ODE TO DYMPHNA*

The poems in *Ode to Dymphna* weave and jolt through the human condition — what it means to inhabit a human body from its cellular to its intricate and holy machinations. They are raw and determined. They are haunting, and in some cases, haunted. They are intentional. They interrogate. They remember. They clap back. In this collection, resilience resonates through the familiar, the mundane, the unpleasant, and the necessary. In her careful eye for image, Belen captures hard truths: mortality is inevitable, these poems teach us, and grief is inevitable, but it is also the warmth of the human condition, in all of its messiness, that sustains us.

— Ariana D. Den Bleyker, founder and publisher of ELJ Editions, Ltd.

In this collection the poet comes into her full power. Biography flaring through into universal message. Meaning. Light. Incandescent and gritty. Not since finding Plath at 17 have I felt this kinship. But more hope here, more humility and love. I'm grateful for these poems. Rest in peace, hopelessness.

— E. K. Gordon, author of "Love Cohoes" and "Walk with Us"
Professor of English, Northampton Community College

Ode to Dymphna is a real feast for thought and, at times, a real punch in the gut. Nina ponders important questions, like bacterial belief systems, and shares more anecdotes captured through the lens of her magnificent wit and humor. This might just be her best work yet!

— Michael A. Carroll, author of "Storm of Summer"
and "Scotch Sympathy"

PRAISE FOR *WARM BLOODED TREE*

Nina Belén Robins writes with gripping authenticity, creating poems that hallmark the human condition. Any reader will relate to the various themes and circumstances illustrated by her words.

— *Cassandra Alfred, author of "This is How You Love Her"*

To use a line from one of her poems, "they've seen me at last," *Warm Blooded Tree* has a way of capturing the vulnerability and desperation in loneliness that many of us are led to believe is unique to only a select few.

In spite of that, so many of Robins' poems paint a poignant picture of the universal craving for connection we all experience, and how the small seemingly insignificant bright spots of contact help to connect us to the humanity and compassion we often take for granted. Her vulnerability and insight into the human condition is arresting, and after reading her most recent book, once again I feel like I have been caught in the embrace of her words.— *Adam Biggs, NPS poet and artist from NY*

Who among us has not known loneliness? Nina Belén Robins' poems in Warm Blooded Tree will creep into the empty spaces that haunt your soul at night and remind you just how human and vulnerable you are. Her adroit ability to weave you into her stories whether you think you belong there or not is as present in her newest book as it was in the three before it. Get ready to experience some feelings with this powerful collection of perspicacious poetry. — *Danni Green poet and singer*

PRAISE FOR *T. GONDII*

Having had the pleasure of reading all three of this author's published books, it is no surprise that she continues to amaze and move me with her poetry. Her collection takes you on a journey, and draws you into her world, full of pain and love, and of course cats! She is an inspiration to me, and I cannot recommend this (and her other two books) highly enough!

— *Deb Klein*

I loved reading this. I especially appreciated "To my Future Mother in Law" and "Consent." Not only is this well written, it makes me feel less alone. I love the raw honesty and total exposure on these pages. Nina perfectly captures so many of the things I've experienced. Reading this felt like sitting down with a friend who gets it.

— *KH*

"Buy the ticket, take the ride" This is an amazing collection of thoughts, struggles and stories of a truly amazing woman. This collection does not disappoint.

— *Thanh Wisler*

T. GONDII

Nina Belén Robins

With searing honesty and ferocious wit, noted poet and mental health advocate Robins Illuminates the brutal internal and external pressure to bear children; and the courage, self-awareness, love— and pain — required to remain child-free. Just when her words become near-unbearable, she throws in a sly and hilarious poem about cats.

available online
in paperback and
ebook format

PRAISE FOR *A BED WITH MY NAME ON IT*

Bookended by movingly hopeful poems, this collection carries the reader into places we may never have been and may hope never to go to. But having been there and come through — with the writer — with humor, deep humanity, and an energizing self-acceptance, we're better for it. These poems have the music of performance poetry in them and the power of crafted literary work. We have here a very satisfying and rare merger of talent, humility and valuable life experience. No poem fell flat for me. Every poem invites and rewards multiple readings. — *Elizabeth K. Gordon*

If you have ever had a moment that made you feel out of control, this book has a poem for you. Several, in fact, and not one of them gives you a feeling of anything less than survival at its finest. Don't forget this poet's name. Nina will have a long career. You won't forget the poetry. — *Wil Gibson*

I read this book in one sitting! Nina brought us into her life and spread light into so many places so often left in the dark. It was a pleasure to share her perspective. I work with girls in a community residence and I could relate to each page with the girls I have worked with as well as my own personal experiences. This was so powerful. — *Amanda*

Nina's book *A Bed with my Name on It* is tragic beauty. The poems are filled with so much raw emotion, each one is like a gut punch of "damn." I'm very grateful for her poems. — *Nick Yuk*

PRAISE FOR *SUPERMARKET DIARIES*

This magnificent volume of poetry is the author's first published book but surely not her last. With impeccable insight and a vivacious appreciation for the human condition, Robins takes us on a journey behind the supermarket check-out counter. She offers us a unique glimpse into the lives of the ordinary people who cross her path each day, using her incredible poetic talents to convince us of the extra-ordinary humanity of each of them, and by extension, of ourselves. I highly recommend this book!

— *choirqueer*

Simple observations, expressed with great insight, wisdom and eloquence.

— *Dan Couture*

In a variety of stories through the eyes of a creatively observant cashier, Nina's writing is sharp witted, emotional, and promises to be very memorable!

— *Zadra*

This is The Spoon River Anthology of supermarkets: insightful poems about customers, staff and life behind the cash register, by an exciting young NYC poet. Can't wait for the next book!

— *Lori Ubell*

SUPER-MARKET DIARIES

Nina Belén Robins

Mild-mannered grocery store employee by day, Nina Robins is a well-known performance poet who has twice performed at the National Poetry Slam. Her poetry has been described as "exceptionally appealing," "heartbreakingly honest," and "subversively deep for work so overtly entertaining."

— Taylor Mali, author of
What Teachers Make

available online
in paperback and
ebook format

Nina Belén Robins is a three-time National Slam Poet, and author of the books of poetry: *Supermarket Diaries, A Bed With My Name On It*, *T. Gondii*, *Warm Blooded Tree*, *Ode to Dymphna*, and *Saturday Morning Serotonin.*

She spent much of her life in various institutions, but has finally broken free and lives with her husband and cats, working in the bakery department of a supermarket.

She writes whenever possible, and wants to help normalize and destigmatize mental illness as best she can.

www.ingramcontent.com/pod-product-compliance
Lightning Source LLC
LaVergne TN
LVHW041235150826
845673LV00008B/2391

* 9 7 9 8 9 8 6 9 3 8 5 2 3 *